Printed in Mexico

ISBN 978-0-15-362194-9

ISBN 0-15-362194-X

7 8 9 10   0908   16 15 14 13 12 11
4500314578

Harcourt
SCHOOL PUBLISHERS

Visit *The Learning Site!*
www.harcourtschool.com

Is It Alive?

Living things grow and change. Living things need food, water, and air. They also need space to grow. A living thing needs all these things to stay alive.

This dog grew from a puppy. It needs food, air, and water every day.

This toy dog does not grow or change over time.

Living things can also make new living things like themselves. Plants, animals, and people are all living things.

Nonliving things are not alive. They do not grow and change. They can not make things from themselves. Which dog is a nonliving thing?

 COMPARE AND CONTRAST How are the dogs in the pictures on these pages different?

Plants and Animals

Plants and animals are two kinds of living things. They meet their needs in different ways. A bear drinks water from a stream and catches fish for food. The bear uses a cave for shelter. **Shelter** is a safe place to live.

The bear needs a lot of space to find food and move around. Smaller animals need less space.

Bears meet their needs for food and water in the wild.

Sunflowers do not catch their food. They use sunlight, air, and water to make their food.

Plants also need space, so their roots and branches can spread out. Plants use sunlight, air, and water to make their own food.

Focus Skill

COMPARE AND CONTRAST How do plants and animals meet their needs for food and water?

Fast Fact

The Venus Fly Trap is not like most plants. It gets some of its food by catching insects!

Growing and Changing

All living things grow and change. A bear mother gives birth to young cubs. The cubs grow bigger and stronger over time. They learn to catch fish and find food from trees and plants to stay alive. Young cubs grow up to look like adult bears.

Adult bears teach their cubs to find food to stay alive.

A sunflower begins as a seed (1).
The young plant grows (2, 3, 4).
Soon, flowers will form.

Sunflowers come from the seeds of mature sunflower plants. The seeds fall to the ground where they get water and food from the soil. Young plants grow from the seeds. As the plants grow, they form flowers and more sunflower seeds.

 MAIN IDEA AND DETAILS How do bear cubs grow and change?

Meeting Needs

Large plants and animals need a lot of food, water, and space. Small animals do not need as much.

Sometimes living things can not meet all of their needs. There may be no water if it has not rained. In winter, food may be hard to find. Animals or plants may run out of places to live.

When it can not find grass to eat, this deer eats the bark from trees.

Young plants and animals may not grow as big or strong as they should. They could die if there is not enough water to drink or places to live. Sometimes living things must find new places to live.

 MAIN IDEA AND DETAILS What could happen if living things do not meet their needs?

Some animals must move from place to place to find enough food and water to live.

Living Things on Earth

Everywhere on Earth there are living things. They grow and change. Trees and plants grow from seeds. Fish, birds, and insects grow from eggs. Each living thing lives in a place where it can meet its needs for food, water, and air.

 COMPARE AND CONTRAST How are all living things alike?

Summary

Living things are different from nonliving things. Plants, animals, and people are all living things. Living things need food, water, air, and space. Animals also need shelter. Plants need the sun to make food. Living things grow and change. If living things do not meet their needs, they may not grow or stay alive.

Places such as this pond meet the needs of many living things.

Glossary

living Growing and changing. Plants and animals are living things because they need food, water, and air. (2, 3, 4, 6, 8, 9, 10, 11)

nonliving Not alive. Air, water, and rocks are nonliving because they do not grow and change. (3, 11)

shelter A safe place to live. Bears may use a cave for shelter. (4)